THE JOURNEY
Without Knowing
God Was
Really There

THE JOURNEY

WITHOUT KNOWING GOD WAS REALLY THERE

VOL. 1&2
GIFTS

with

OSCAR DIXON, SR

PTP

Pure Thoughts Publishing, LLC

DEDICATION

Rev. Frank D. Dixon Mrs. Ethel M. Dixon

During my youth, I don't remember home life with an uncomfortable lifestyle; our parents had a harmonious relationship. I don't remember loud boisterous voices and disagreements coming through the house in the midst of seven children.

My innocence betrayed me as I grew older: what I was experiencing was not the norm in other homes; we had hard times, shortages of everything, but the love of our parents for us and the Lords, words can't describe.

My dad and mother were always hugging and playing with us, and I didn't know it then, but there were spiritual blessings of impartation placed on our lives. We grew up passing on to our children what we received from our parents, the Lord of their lives, is the Lord of our lives, and we believe the Lord brought the parents up the rough side of the mountain and set them on a solid foundation in Christ Jesus the Solid Rock, and so it is with us. I so dedicate these writings and testimonies to our parents and sisters and brothers; to tell the story is to be in concert with our upbringing.

THE JOURNEY WITHOUT KNOWING GOD WAS REALLY THERE

The Journey Begins: Vol.1

INTRODUCTION

My Journey; Not Knowing God; Was Really There

THE WRITING OF THIS BOOK IS A SPIRITUAL FOCUS.

I.   I. MY JOURNEY; WITHOUT KNOWING GOD; WAS REALLY THERE

My journey began in my youth, as early as I can remember, with my father and mother, two sisters and four brothers. It continues today, and I have taken stock and realized that the Lord Jesus Christ is my present help.

II.   I SURRENDER ALL:

Things were happening to me, and for me. I am trying to take inventory of my life. I knew in my heart that Mother was gone to glory and now Dad as well has been called home. Early one Sunday morning the Lord gave me this song, "I SURRENDER ALL." I realize going forward perhaps I would be going through spiritual cleansing. My writing is of the Lord, and I must be clear and balanced in my work.

III. FOR, I AM DOING A NEW THING:

When I read this scripture, Isaiah 43:18-19, the presence of the Holy Spirit was so fulfilling. I was in tears, the Lord was speaking. The System Operator at the Rehabilitation Center gave me that scripture to read. The scripture represents The Lord Exodus out of Egypt as enormous with Moses, but the Lord is saying now, that was minor compared to what is coming.

Chapter One

THE JOURNEY BEGINS

THE EARLY YEARS

I: Ephesians 1:4: (NIV) For He chose us in Him before the creation to be holy and blameless in His sight.

TRANSLATION:

For us, salvation is of God, not us. The mystery of salvation originated in the timeless mind of God long before we existed. Because of Christ, we are holy and blameless in His sight. God chooses us, and when we belong to Him through Jesus Christ, God looks at us as if we had never sinned. All we need is to continue to praise Him for His wonderful love.

ONCE UPON A TIME I would have asked, why am I here? After many years, I realized that I am part of His plan from before the beginning of time.

When I came to know myself, I was very young and had a wandering mind that I call very curious and always alert. I wondered how things and objects worked, and that curiosity led me to examining things of which I often broke or misplaced. I was very young, perhaps six or seven, and my dad was holding a very expensive watch for a church member. We were told not to touch, which meant to me I can examine it and see how it works, and it was soon in pieces and my mother wanted a piece of me, but Dad said, "Ethel Mae, don't touch that boy," and that was it and no debate. I felt guilty about that for a long time afterward, because there was no way to repair the damage and my disobedience.

When I had done something wrong, I was very frightened about what would happen when our parents came home. Then I realized early in my youth that our parents were very kind parents that are filled with a humility that I couldn't understand. My dad was a quiet man, with a kind presence, and was easy to communicate with. He was 6' 2" and 260 pounds, with a low voice and his eyes perhaps would search your face quietly. It is said before you say anything, think about it and let your conscious be your guide. There were times I knew the Bible states spare the rod and spoil the child, because my dad always found the good in everything you did and he didn't make you feel small but enhanced your self-esteem

Through the years, Mother and Father always encouraged us to have our own business and this way you will always have choices. You can't imagine what that sounds like to a 9- or 10-year-old with four brothers and two older sisters. As children of a sharecropper and a Methodist Minister of A.M.E. Zion Churches, we had to move occasionally. One so young would dare to dream that such opportunities could exist back in the 1950s.

My dad, the Rev. Frank Dixon, was a very humble man, he worked in our communities very quietly and was sought out for many needs in our communities. When families were in need of prayer, spiritual direction, food for their families and somewhere to stay, Rev. Dixon was always at the helm and performed a tremendous task, and was tireless in his devotion to help others. In my sight, my dad and mom stood taller than anyone I knew. I love the manner in which he approached his tasks. Whatever he did and for whoever he did it for, it was never mentioned again.

Times for us during my youth was trying because as sharecroppers we could barely make ends meet. I would be with Dad sometimes and he would meet someone or they would stop by the house and he'd find a way to share out of the very little we had. Ethel Mae and Frank believed God would always make a way somehow. As a matter of fact, this was one of his favorite songs. In my younger years, Dad seemed to always be in a giving or a surrendering attitude to help others.

Ephesians 1:4 (NIV)

> For He chose us in Him before the creation of the world to be holy and blameless in his sight.

TRANSLATION:

> For us, salvation is of God, not of us. The mystery of salvation originated in the timeless mind of God long before we existed. Because of Christ, we are holy and blameless in His sight. God chooses us, and when we belong to Him through Jesus Christ, God looks at us as if we had never sinned. All we need to do is to continue to praise Him for his wonderful love.

Messages in Our Dreams

Proverbs 16:1-3, vs.1) The preparations of the heart in man, and the answer of the tongue, is from the Lord. vs.2) All the ways of a man are clean in His eyes; but the Lord weighted the spirits. vs.3) Commit thy works unto the Lord, and thy thoughts shall be established.

Translation: vs.1) The renewing grace of God alone prepares the heart for every good work. This teaches us that we are not sufficient of ourselves tithing or speak anything wise and good. vs.2) Ignorance, pride, and self-flattery render us partial judges respecting our own conduct. vs.3) Roll the burden of thy care upon God, and leave it with Him, by faith and dependence on Him.

I had made several attempts to call and speak with my long-time family friend, Laura, to tell her she has been in my dreams. In this dream, she said, "she intended to tell me something." I recognized her voice in the dream, and this song came into my spirit, "The Lord Wants It All." I recognized the song, as it was very popular at this time in our culture; the artist that wrote and produced this powerful invitation with direction to the Lord, He can provide all that we need. I began humming this song in my mind, over and over until I fell asleep.

When I had gotten up that morning, a strange thing had happened: the Lord had given me a message for someone in my dream, He gave me a name and what He wanted and how much, "He Wants It All."

Stranger than strange, I began humming another song that came into my spirit while I was working, I began humming, "I Surrender All." I knew there was a message in this song for me, it had come up in my spirit before, I didn't need a commentary to exegete "surrender all." I had already begun more prayer, fasting, Bible Study and Sunday school, then I realized that I needed growth, to give up much of my daily work and follow his assignments.

I needed answers. I decided if I didn't get an answer to my call I would travel to see her, so we could share in the mysteries of our dreams from on high, the dream that had disturbed me, and left me very concerned, because I hadn't heard from her.

A few days later she answered the phone and we talked for a few minutes, then she told me about waking up very early in the morning, uncomfortable and alone. I began to realize the loss of her friend, in spite of the time passed, had not settled with her. As she talked, I felt in my spirit and suggested to her, she had been hearing my name in her dreams, yet hadn't responded or called me. Laura replied that my name had been in her dreams a few times. I said why don't we share, I am going through some issues myself, I have not resolved them yet.

A few months ago I visited you, and as we talked, I believe the Lord was saying to me, he had something for you to do.

I am informing you now, the Lord has a calling on your life, "Your journey begins now, the Lord will direct you because you have already spoken of people contacting you for various help in several situations. I am always available to you, any time you call I will answer; to call is up to you. You know we grew up together and went to school and we have earned each other's trust over all these years.

When we talked, I felt the Holy Spirit's presence. When I welcomed Him and was led into prayer, I felt a fresh anointing go out to her. I called forth comforting angels be sent to her and abide as her comforter, as promised. While praying, the song I had been humming in my dream, turned out be her favorite song, "The Lord Wants It All." Often the messages in our dreams and visions are given by the Lord to lead and guide us and teach us how to grow daily and become dependent upon the Lord.

Chapter Two

THE EARLY YEARS CONTINUE

Psalm 37:26; They are always generous and lend freely, their children will be blessed.

THERE WAS A TIME in which I remember that we had a bountiful harvest of corn, cotton, and a prosperous garden. My older sisters and brothers had harvested the crops and they were stored in the barn, and if things had gone according to plan, the cotton would have been hauled to the cotton gin and milled. As bad timing would have it, along came Oscar into the barn where Gus and Gordon were shucking corn and Oscar came in playing with matches and set the barn on fire, burning up all the cotton with everything else, and nearly burned up Gus, Gordon and myself. Fortunately for us, the Lord loves Rev. Dixon, and He promised us in His Word, He always makes us a way to escape when there seems to be no way out. There was a large plank in the back of the barn that was a little loose and Louis and James discovered it and broke it open and we all climbed out the back of the barn. By then it was fully ablaze and we barely escaped with our lives. Thank you, Jesus.

When we all assembled in the house and Dad arrived home, I was so frightened for an overly inquisitive little boy who expected to get himself the whipping of the year, and well deserved. Once again, the peace and the serenity of my dad prevailed and there was no capital punishment metered out to the little rascal.

There was a spiritual harmony that prevailed that day, a powerful move of The Lord that left that plank board loose enough to be knocked open, and the Holy Spirit touched our dad to let him know there was danger on the home front. When he had arrived home, the barn had burned down, as well as everything in it except his three boys; the Lord Jesus had protected us, for even then he had a plan for our lives.

Jeremiah 29:11(NIV) "For I know the plans I have for you," declares the Lord, "plans to prosper you and not harm you, plans to give you hope and a future." There were parts that I didn't remember so clearly, so I talked with my sister, Miriam, and she helped me to recapture some of my early years. When dad arrived home and saw the barn was a heap of smoldering ashes, his greatest concern was, were his children safe? I couldn't imagine how difficult it was to replace the barn, and the farm crop for the year that was meant to help feed us through the winter and to pay the borrowed money back for a failed crop, which is usually borrowed against having a successful harvest. I was quite young when this happened, but my head seemed to be angled at the ground, as I was ashamed to look others in the face. Even now, the tears keep coming down as I write this. I thank the Lord for our dad; he gave me the courage to lift my head from the shame.

There was something about this man, this Rev. Frank Dixon, who was so humble and yet had a presence that commanded a certain respect when he appeared in the presence of others. It appeared that other parents' children loved our father. I would be with him sometimes and when other parents' children saw him, they rushed out to the edge of the road and greeted him as we would be walking home. If he stopped and chatted with them, they stared after him like he was the only friend they ever had and I didn't question what seemed so obvious. I thought that kind of warmth, kindness, and patience were reserved for his children only. I didn't know then the terminology, but that was a character like Jesus that just drew children to him and they were never the same afterward. I didn't know then that the blessing that was upon him from the Holy Spirit, led him along these roadways and had blessed him to help others with a word from the Lord.

Most children that reached out to him, their parents were better off than we were because we were sharecroppers. I reflected on this as we walked up the sandy, hot, and dusty road, to the Wright Community, southwest of Tuskegee where we lived at that time.

> Psalm 37:26 (NIV) They are all ways generous and lend freely, their children will be blessed.

TRANSLATION:

> There are unfortunate exceptions to this general principle: God provides for his own people. The children of the righteous need not go hungry because other believers can help out in their time of need.

THE EARLY YEARS CONTINUE II

> Ephesian 1: 4; According as he hath chosen us in him before the foundation of the world, that we should be holy and without blame before him in love.

This positive affect our dad and mom had on other families and there children sometime created a tenderness towards jealousy by his children.

Dad travel to New York to visit with his sons and daughters, he came to my house and spent the night. The next morning I was leaving with my pick-up truck and chains saws to take down small trees for a co-worker.

A little to my surprise, dad wanted to come along with me so we could perhaps spend some quality time together. I had not been home in a few years. We arrived at the property, we were invited into the house I introduced my dad to my friend, his wife and two teenage daughters.

I left home a few years ago, I had forgotten how quickly young people had immediate attachment to my father. I thought he was coming outside with me and watch my handiwork, I was about to take down couple trees, trim them up and cut them into fire wood. I look around for him several times he was no where in site.

I went inside to check on dad to make certain he didn't feel abandon, when I walked in the door, the wife and daughters had him covered. He was sitting in there dad's favorite big chair with a fresh cup of coffee near by and the two daughters sitting on the floor, one on each side leaning on him and they were engulfed in perhaps one of his best bible stories that he could teach so eloquently, they were spellbound.

I went back outside alone, even the father was leaning on the wall taken by his friendship and the ministry my father was call to by our Lord and Savior Jesus Christ. Family, we are losing many of our children to school dropout that often leads to imprisonment. I pray that each of us such our hearts on how can we bring positive impact to help save the lives of our future. I am going to follow my calling, I believe this way I can impart into others lives, just by following my calling trying to fulfilled the purpose the Lord has for me. I have met and work with many young people while serving on my street ministry over the pass 13 or 14 years. In this moment, I bless each and everyone who is striving to be more like Christ Jesus everyday.

A few years later, dad passed, and the news came to me, I informed my job and when my friend saw me and gave his condolences he was visibly shaken and his wife and daughters shed tears when they heard about there friend. I pray that the journey we are on for the Lord, be one that enhance the lives of others.

TRANSLATION:

> This was from the choice of them in Christ, before the foundation of the world, that they should be made holy by separation from sin, being set apart to God, and sanctified by the Holy Spirit, in consequence of their election in Christ.

Chapter Three

MY YOUTH I

Deut: 33:23; Let me be satisfied with favor and filled with Your blessing.

TRANSLATION:

We should not only invite others to the service of God, but abound in it. The Blessing of Naphtali. The favor of God is the only favor satisfying to the soul. Those are happy indeed, who have the favor of God; and those shall have it, who reckon that in having it they have enough, and desire no more.

TRYING TO PUT ME in a particular role in my youth was difficult at best. I was a busy little rascal, and working to please my dad or mom was alright with me. I was a very good babysitter. I was helpful around the kitchen, especially when it was time to prepare for dinner; I wanted my food to smell like mother's one day. I was probably ten or eleven, and I would get the water buckets and head down to the water spring and bring fresh water for Mother to prepare for the evening and dinner. Helping Mother, I enjoyed learning to cook fairly well, so when Mother left for visits, I was the cook.

There was something about this man, Rev. Frank, who was so humble and yet had a presence that commanded a certain respect when he appeared in the presence of others. I didn't know at the time about being filled with the Holy Ghost, not at that young age. I would be with him sometimes and when other parents' children saw him they rushed out to the edge of the road and greeted him, as we would be walking home. On one occasion the children saw Rev. Frank coming, they ran out to the road and wrapped their little arms around his legs and wouldn't let go.

I knew we had a right to love our dad and mom, but well-off parents' children ran to him like he was the only friend they had ever seen. It didn't make sense to me walking home barefoot in the hot sand. On these occasions, he reached in his handkerchief and gave each a coin, as if they needed financial help. Then he picked them up and walked them back inside the gate and greeted their mother, who had a sad continent about her, barely a smile for the Rev. Frank. He said something to her, I thought, and she began to smile, and a few minutes later she had this radiant smile, and thanked him for stopping.

I didn't know then that the blessing that were upon him from the Holy Spirit led him along these roadways and had blessings for others with a word from the Lord.

This is a small glimpse into our family challenges, with our eldest sister Miriam's life. When she was in the 5th grade, doing well with her grades, the teacher decided not to pass her to the 6th grade. Daddy relocated us, and she went to the 6th grade, but she had the same problem in the 7th grade and it had to be worked out. We wondered, what made our family life difficult by others? We had no real understanding. Often our dad would adjust and move to another location. We knew if he raised up the name of the Lord and declared something against someone, it would be unhealthy. I still hurt how we are treated today. I know we weren't the only ones who had to fight against these kinds of obstructions, so I prayed for others then and now, and thank our Lord for sustaining us, giving us peace in our storms—they never go away, but we get stronger because of them.

Remember, if there is a battle to be fought, no matter what kind, don't go without our Lord Jesus Christ. He is our covenant care in all things, and the Lord promised to fight our battles if we trust him to do so. I can tell you He is my saving grace from my early youth until these days where the gray hair can be seen. May the Lord of us all continue to protect us.

Chapter Four

MY YOUTH II

Proverb 20:7 (KJV) The just man walketh in his integrity: his children are blessed after him.

I DEVELOPED CONFIDENCE FROM the hands-on assistance from my new teacher, and her patience and support. On Friday evening, minutes before school would turn out, she would call me to her desk and remind me to cut the lawn on Saturday. I believe she was looking into my empty pockets and new I couldn't rub two dimes together, I was that broke.

My new teacher hired me to cut their lawn on Saturday morning and whatever other work they needed to be done. Cutting the lawn consisted of pushing the old-fashioned lawn mower. The lawn was very small with old Bermuda grass, which is the only stuff that would grow in this heat in that area.

When I left the community school, we were bused to Adam Junior High School. This was quite a distance from home. Needless to say, this was in the 50s and segregation was alive and well in the South. I don't remember exactly how many Caucasian schools we passed, but there should have been at least two. I confess that I had some very long days, riding the school bus pass two other schools and having to receive our school's books from those schools after several years of their use. I either heard or was asked if I wanted to sacrifice my one-hour lunch to work in the kitchen cleaning up pots, pans, and dishes for a meal after everyone had eaten. I wasn't ready for what came next: the head cooked took what meats were left and put them aside to take home for her family, I would suppose. If it was a good day, she would give me a spoon of mashed potatoes and cabbage or collard greens. In hindsight, I believe my favorite teacher put my name out there in order to help me survive the long days at school by working for food. I know this is true now, as I pend this to the Lord. I began to cry; early in my life the Lord made a way not only for me but my sisters and brothers.

I kept this simple, I said to myself, the Lord did this because He answers my mom and dad's prayers. I will inform you faint-hearted ones and faithful saints alike, I had to learn to get it right for my-self. I turned around one day and both parents had passed. I had to learn to look into the hills, whence cometh my help, it comes from the Lord, so I became a seeker of the Lord who can do all things. I needed a new friend, someone who wouldn't put me in a category. I know men still do, but God, He is my personal friend and my joy.

This school registered seventh and eighth graders from many different areas, for this was a public school. The other elementary school students that had parents better financially suited had established private schools for their children to attend. This was not totally clear to me until many years later how these schools were developed and who attended them. When I graduated seventh and eighth grade we went on to high school at Tuskegee Institute.

I realized early in life the playing field wasn't equal, or fair, and I had to find a place within me to send the debris so I wouldn't get clutter and let it make me angry and unhappy. I was so young in high school, trying to get past the favorite student and the not-so-favorite in school, and workplace. My dad stepped up to the plate and handed me a Bible and told me to always keep this in my car, visible for others to see. Listen, family, I learned as I read the

Bible from cover to cover, and listened to Dr. Martin Luther King. Remember, my stepping stone was a solid foundation, with this, I had a place to stand.

> Proverb 20:7 (KJV.) The just man walketh in his integrity; his children are blessed after him.

TRANSLATION:

> I believe it is a wonderful heritage to have an honest father. He will teach you his way, and you will walk in them; we become kingdom children.

Chapter Five

MY YOUTH III

THE JOURNEY BEGINS

Psalm 35:27 (vs.27) Let them shout for joy, and be glad, that favor my righteous cause: Yea, let them say continually, Jehovah be magnified, Who hath please in the prosperity of his servants.

TRANSLATION:

They trust their souls in His hands, they are one with Him by faith, are precious in His sight, and shall be rescued from destruction, that they may give thanks in heaven.

I GREW UP IN the surrounding area of Tuskegee. I don't know for certain, but the name of this southern town and the people of the times unevenly matched. If you saw the agriculture working at the university, you would say, there is something going on for the benefit of our communities, and for individuals to learn how to grow our animals with proper feeding. New feed products were out that were very good for milk cows. This special clover when the cows had grazing time made the cows healthier and they produced more milk.

I suppose this grazing information perhaps wouldn't reach our table when eating dinner and having a discussion of the times and what is current and beneficial for us as farming sharecroppers. This knowledge was beneficial for us as sharecroppers; it so happens the farm we worked on, there was this professor who worked at the university, and he acquired knowledge how to grow this product when it was ready for the cows to feed. It was my job to help get them in the clover field.

As I reveal these formative years about Oscar, somehow I was made the designated worker to help the professor feed his milk cows and assist him in milking them. I was the timekeeper who let the cows into the clover field late evening and after a short while, I removed them. I learned that this clover feeding was very healthy: it cleansed their blood, helped with digestion, and early the next morning, the yield was excellent.

Here is the blessing in the analogy of sharecropping and it was generally understood, if this was what your family did, you were one hot summer or a rainy season that produced a poor crop and you couldn't feed the family, or pay your one year boarding fee. Sometime if you had a bad crop, you had to make good for both years if you were allowed to stay. Since I was the designate helper for the professor, on rare occasions I called up my dad's milk cows and let them graze as well.

I could be lying; I don't remember the professor ever telling me I couldn't share this blessed food with my dad's cows, as a matter of fact. Notes should have been dropped in mail boxes to let others know.

Reverend Frank did much work in the surrounding communities, often the customers didn't have the funds to pay him. They went down to the barn and selected a calf or couples of pigs and gifted them to Dad. They drove him home in their pickup truck with the gifts.

I hope my family are getting the message, "This was bread from heaven, feed me till I want know more." I believe, many families experience these times, poor crops from heat and rain, but we have our "Father" in heaven who answer prayers and feeds us from his abundance. We were always taught that our Reverend Frank had this great relationship with the Lord. When the weather with heat and rain hadn't been kind to us, Dad and Mom would be praying for rain. Then the bottom fell out, with great rain from heaven.

Reverend Frank, would walk out into the backyard and make a declaration to "Our God," Lord let rain fall upon our crop in the early rain, and save some for our crops in the latter rain, it will need rain as well, Thank You Lord, it is already done, in your name, you are glorified.

Chapter Six

NOBODY LIKE YOU LORD

(THE JOURNEY BEGINS)

Philippians 4:8

> Finally, brethren, whatsoever things are true, whatsoever things are honest, whatsoever things are just, whatsoever things are pure, whatsoever things are lovely, whatsoever things are of good report; if there be any virtue, and if there be any praise, think on these things.

TRANSLATION:

> Philippians 4:8 Let believers be of one mind, and ready to help each other. As the apostle had found the benefit of their assistance, he knew how comfortable it would be to his fellow-laborers to have the help of others. Let us seek to give assurance.

EARLY THIS MORNING I was up after 05:00 a.m. for prayer and meditation, and while in meditation, I had a vision, this quick flash of a hand came across my stomach going toward the left side. I had been praying for the Holy Spirit to bless me with angels of healing that they would breathe on me and touch me with wellness. Those who know me, know I am very active in my works and what other functions I am engaged in.

While meditating that morning, I had my hickory walking stick, the Lord calls my rod and staff. I had it laying across my body from left foot, and I heard this voice say, in two weeks your circulation is done. There is a take away from this event in my daily walk with Christ, He has blessed me in so many ways beyond what I deserve. We can't fight the devil by ourselves, we need to be filled with the Holy Spirit and lined up with prayer warriors of faith. I feel the Holy Spirit almost to tears when I review this.

One morning while in meditating I had been in prayer to the Lord to help me overcome my sin nature; it seemed like I was always in chastisement from the Lord. I had been reading scriptures and commentaries for a full meaning so I could walk in right standing with the Lord. Family, I am an avid reader of the Word of God, I believe and trust the Word.

When I finished reading Philippians 4:8, I put it under my pillow, and I asked the Holy Spirit to help me bring this into my spirit and heart to remembrance and grow from my sinful action. In my vision, the Lord taught me something. The paper was under my pillow, and I see in my vision this hand snatch this folded paper from under my pillow. At first I thought the Lord was helping me, but He showed me when we aren't solid in our spiritual walk, with Christ, the word has fallen on shallow ground and the enemy steals it.

For me, this intense effort to get the word of God into all who is wondering, does the Holy Spirit answer prayers, does he truly live in your life, can I hear from him when I need an answer to my fears and sorrows. Be encouraged the testimonies and scriptures with translation is witnessing for the non-believer and the one who is sitting on the fence, and had bad experiences with getting answers back from the Lord. Wait I say, wait, on the Lord. Daniel waited, factually speaking, and while he waited, because of his faith, he knew the Lord would answer. He went on a 21-day fast and prepared himself for the blessing he believed would come. Daniel 10:2; In those days I, Daniel, was mourning three full weeks.

THE JOURNEY WITHOUT KNOWING GOD WAS REALLY THERE

Vol. 2: Gifts

PREFACE

FOR I AM DOING A NEW THING:

ISAIAH 43: 18-19 Vs.18 (Forget the former things; do not dwell on the past. Vs.19) See, I am doing a new thing! Now it springs up: do you not perceive it? I am making a way in the desert and streams in the wasteland.

TRANSLATION:

This scripture pictures a new exodus for a people once again oppressed, as the Israelites had been as slaves in Egypt before the exodus. They would cry to God, and again He would hear and deliver them. A new exodus would take place through a new desert. The past miracles were nothing compared to what God would do for His people in the future.

WHEN I LOOK BACK on yester-years, I am learning to look at my growth, my footprint where the Lord has and is still placing them. In my youth I walked home from the little jobs, cutting lawns on the Tuskegee Institute. For a young man of 15 through 18, I worked very long hours and it was dangerous walking home along the highway.

It was an extremely long walk home, especially at 6:00 or 7:00

p.m. after having a paper route before school in the morning and a full day of school and then walking home, which was over 7 or 8 miles, after cutting a large lawn.

As I walked alone, I day-dreamed of traveling abroad to foreign nations, such as Greece, to look on the ruins of Rome, and to walk in the waters of my ancestors in South Africa. Travel into Elmira of West Africa and stand in the exit door of the Slave Mansion where the slaves were forced into slave ships, taking them from their home-land and shipping them all over the world.

I have done Mission Trips abroad and Outreach Missions locally in our states, and I pray this kind of work has to do with reaching and ministering to the unchurched, connecting the past with the new. Through all of this, Our Lord and Savior Christ Jesus was and continues to be in all things. When I was reading this to Prophetess Miriam, I felt the Holy Spirit's presence in my last statement.

Chapter One

GIFTS ARE OF GOD

Hebrew 1:2 (NIV) But in these last days he has spoken to us
by his Son, whom he appointed.

WHEN I RECEIVED THIS card, the information on it touched me
deeply and brought me to tears: He's the Light of the World;
Worthy One; Emmanuel; God is With Us; The Shepherd; Prince
of Peace; Jesus The Word; The Risen One. The Lord is telling me
I am all these things to you in your life.

My mother called in 1976 and talked with me. Her voice had
been clear and precise, and it said to me she was doing well tonight,
because she had been very sick. I received this divine comment
from her.

She saw the well, with prophets from old times in groups, large
and small groups. "God appeared to her in a natural man and
touched her hand and said, He will never leave her and asked her
if He could use her life to save others, she said I have no life, it is
Yours to do with as You please. This Man said to her, that you stand
taller than all the people I have met, pass this on to your family to
be more consecrated to God. She said I want one of my children to
stay where God can use them. The things you have envisioned have

been enhanced to do even greater things." I received this in 1976 and I have read it recently on July 5, 2009, and The Holy Spirit filled me to tears when I read this powerful testimony coming from my mother. We lost her in August 1977, and I remember many years before her passing, the Lord gave her a vision for the Annual Conference that was beginning in South Atlantic District where my father was a pastor. I remember my dad, Reverend Frank D. Dixon, said Mother told him her vision from the Lord and what He put in her spirit, and she wanted him to inform the Bishops that the Lord had spoken to her for the small local pastors. He said, Ethel Mae the Lord gave this to you, come to the conference with me and you tell them what the Lord said to you. She made her appearance in the Annual Conference many years ago and announced that the Lord put it on her heart to tell the Bishops, prepare now a pension for their local ministers, for when they retire and are unable to work anywhere, they will have a small check coming into their home to help them survive. We know the Lord was in His word because it was put in place and started, to my knowledge this hadn't been spoken until then.

GIFTS IS OF GOD

Hebrew 1:2 (NIV) But in these last days he has spoken to us by his Son, whom he appointed.

TRANSLATION:

Go first to God for advice, talk to him in prayer and listen to him in his Word. He can sustain you in times of stress. From that perspective, you can evaluate all the other wisdom and help made available to you. He can come to us in many ways as His name suggests.

Chapter Two

THE LORD CALLS

(OSCAR BATTLEFIELD)

Judges 7:7 (NIV) The Lord said to Gideon, "With three hundred men that lapped I will save you and give the Midianites into your hands."

I ALWAYS TRY TO prepare mentally and spiritually when I'm going to my church. Our pastor brings very powerful messages, and I have been blessed by them so many times. I have gotten words of direction from his messages. I attend Shaw Temple with expectation and to join in on praise and worship.

There are times I come into church, I just don't feel like standing and singing; the issues and life situations are pressing on me. I have heard it preached and prayed, this is the time we have high praise for the Holy Spirit, for he is the one who can do all things and turn things around, we must trust God.

The pastor was preaching Judges 7:1-8 with Gideon preparing for battle, when he was armed with over 30,000 soldiers, but the Lord had other plans. He speaks to Gideon and tells him he has too many soldiers and would need to reduce his huge numbers of soldiers to a smaller number. The Lord wanted to make certain that his glory wouldn't be stolen from him by the Israelites, and they reduced the number again and again until they were left with only 300 soldiers. Gideon had acted on the plan that the Lord had given him, on choosing the 300 soldiers with faith. When I heard this statement, I felt the Unction of the Holy Ghost.

As the pastor continued to preach, he said in his sermon, someone is here today, that the Lord has called on to "The Battlefield." I was drawn to tears and was just overwhelmed by His presence from that statement. The presence of the Holy Spirit was so fulfilling that I could hardly breathe, I just wept in His sweet presence.

Jacob encountered the Holy Spirit of God and wrestled with him until near daybreak. The angel couldn't wrestle free, and he touched Jacob in the hollow of his thigh and it became out of joint the rest of his life; he walked with a limp. The scriptures say Jacob still didn't let go and said to the angel, "I won't let you go until you bless me." On that statement, I was convicted to tears. This I don't understand, but I am certain it will reveal itself. This statement has given me strength when my health issues are challenging me. The Lord clearly has called me into ministry for Himself and I said yes, now I pray all the more and fast often for understanding in order to learn how to be led by the Holy Spirit.

THE LORD CALLS:

> Judges 7:7 (NIV) The Lord said to Gideon, "With three hundred men that laped I will save you and give the Midianites into your hands."

TRANSLATION:

> The Lord wanted to make certain the Israelites knew it was the power of the Lord that gave the Midianites into their hands, when He reduced them from over 30,000 to 300 men. With a small number of men by the Israelites, it was no doubt God gave them the victory, there were no issues

knowing the glory belonged to God and God alone. We must recognize the danger of fighting in our own strength. We can be confident of victory against life's challenges and temptations only if we put our confidence in God and not ourselves.

Chapter Three

THE KEYS

Matthew 16:19 (NIV) I will give you the keys of the kingdom of heaven, whatever you bind on earth will be bound in heaven, and whatever you loose on earth will be loosed in heaven.

A FEW YEARS AGO, perhaps eight or nine years, I was sitting in my pickup truck down at my barn. It was a very hot afternoon, so I backed my truck underneath the awning as it was cooler under there. I opened my truck doors and had prayer. I was going through health issues at the time. While sitting in my truck, all at once, I saw myself sitting in an old-fashioned desk chair circling high above my barn in the air. I looked down, and there was my barn beneath me and it was so amazing. Just a few minutes before the amazing flight in the chair, I was in this vision and saw the kingdom building with large rooms, with very tall doors, room after room all shining with a golden glow.

Just recently, I had a similar vision, I was in a large building, all golden with tall doors, shining with a glitter to behold, and you can be certain it belongs to our Father who is in heaven. I am not certain what this means that the Holy Spirit allowed me to see such an extraordinary sight and behold just a token of what He has for us. In this year, my West- African pastor and his wife came down to visit me, and the pastor's wife had a word for me; she said the Lord gave me the key. I quickly realized I saw the doors but didn't have the key to open the doors and enter in. By now, I was thoroughly frightened by the sighting of looking into the heavens. When the Holy Spirit showed me the doors and gave someone else the keys to the doors, this was an extraordinary event in my life's journey with the Lord.

THE KEYS:

> Matthew: 16:19 (NIV) I will give you the keys of the kingdom of heaven; whatever you bind on earth will be bound in heaven, and whatever you loose on earth, will be loosed in heaven.

TRANSLATION:

> The meaning of keys to the kingdom has been used in the authority to carry out church discipline, legislation, and administration. Others say the keys give the authority to announce the forgiveness of sin and still others say the keys may be the opportunity to bring people to the kingdom of heaven by presenting them with the message of salvation found in God's Word.

The keys to the kingdom, which are the authority of the Lord and work towards the building of God's Kingdom.

Chapter Four

HE SPEAKS THROUGH OUR DREAMS

I Samuel 1:11 (NIV) And she made a vow, saying. "0 Lord Almighty" if you will only look upon your servant's misery and remember me, and not forget your servant but give her a son, then I will give him to the Lord for all the days of his life, and no razor shall ever be used on his head.

TRANSLATION:

Be careful what you promise in prayer because God may take you up on it. Although we aren't in a position to barter with God, he may still choose to answer a prayer that has an attached promise.

I HAVE JUST COME off a day fasting in the afternoon, and during this time, I was seeking and praying many days and nights, looking for answers to my dreams, visions, and prompting from the Holy Spirit. These lessons were a foundation for me because I continued reading my bible, staying in prayer and fasting for my answers.

Late Tuesday night, early Wednesday morning, I was asleep and this dream began. It was unusual for me; I was having an alcoholic beverage and my mother, it seemed to be her, came to me and took the beverage and poured it out. I was angry, because it seemed to me in the dream, someone was always bothering me.

The next thing I realized, I was sitting on a couch with my head down. I was bewildered and there stood a baby in the fireplace. I quickly realized it was a fireplace because it was large and had white bricks from burning wood. The baby walked from the fireplace to me and said, "I Am Going To Heal You," and the baby walked back into the fireplace. Although there was no fire in the fireplace, I was perplexed at such a scene and comment. Later that same morning, I was reading I Samuel 1:11 and it convicted me to tears when the Holy Spirit filled me with his presence and I wept, for I was unable to hold back my tears. I don't fully understand the scripture in a relationship with the baby coming out of the fireplace. I was in great discomfort, the word that spoke of healing to me was great news and I had hope.

I read Samuel 1:17; Then Eli answered and said, go in peace: and the God of Israel grant thee thy petition that thou hast asked of Him. There were times when my life was in storms, it seemed they would never end, and the Lord answered my prayers through dreams, and scriptures. When the Word came, it was overwhelming and brought me to tears when "The Holy Spirit of God" would touch me and brought me hope and I would be filled to overflow.

This particular morning the Holy Spirit was upon me as I read the scriptures, I am now in I Samuel 3:8; and the Lord called Samuel again the third time. He arose and went to Eli and said here am I; for thou didst call me. Eli perceived that the Lord had called the child. I was saying yes also to God, because I was filled with tears, and later I had to revisit how long ago did the Lord really call me. My sister Miriam suggested very strongly to find out from the Lord how long ago did He call me to serve Him. Through prayer the Lord revealed to me, he had called me at the tender age of 14 down in lower Tuskegee, riding with my dad and his friend, Rev. Robert. I didn't hear clearly in my younger years, but answered His call in my early sixties. For me, this is going through a serious test by the Lord, testing me to see if I can be used in His service, and can I be trusted with His Word and His Children. I believe He is telling me through Isaiah that He called me several times and I failed to answer. Now that I have said yes, will you trust the Lord no matter how bad it gets, how bad it looks, and feel, will you still stand on the promises of God.

I am still standing because the Lord is the truth and the light and there is no coming to the Father but by Him.

Chapter Five

I SURRENDER ALL

OSCAR'S SONG

Romans 6:13 (NIV) Do not offer parts of your body to sin, as instruments of wickedness but rather offer yourselves to God, as those who have been brought from death to life, and offer the parts of your body to Him as instruments of righteousness.

IN MY PRAYERS TO The Holy Spirit, I committed to spending more meaningful time with Him. After prayer, my mother-in-law was just beginning to prepare her breakfast and she commented that the great grandbaby had woke her up by getting into her bed. As she told me what had happened with her, I felt the prompting of The Holy Spirit and went in and prayed a prayer of healing upon his every need. The Holy Spirit's presence was so strong that the baby woke up, turned over and looked at me in the midst of my prayer and went back to sleep. After the prayer, I was not certain it was for healing of his health, and thank God today, he speaks normal and is very healthy. His mother and father worked so diligently with him as he came through with the blessing of God upon him.

When I write of my testimonies, they are painful, but our Holy Spirit promises to bless others through the testimonies of myself and others. The Holy Spirit came to me early this morning around 02:00 a.m. and touched me in my right side and I heard in my spirit that I had a problem in my colon. I have wondered why bad news seemed to come very early in the morning; this touch left me frightened to a point I broke out in a sweat and I wondered what was going on.

Recently, as three months prior, I had my colonoscopy, and all was well. I am to believe I was being chastised and would gain strength through this ordeal. I confess today, in my prayers I believe The Holy Spirit gave me the courage to endure and He placed an angel about me to protect me while I got better. Through my experiences, without the hand of The Holy Ghost upon me, going through your trials you don't want to be in it without The Holy Spirit, because He is our hope, the prayer warriors will be called and there will be words of inspiration that will pick you up when you need it most.

I was reading a book by Lysa Terkeurst, in which she tells the story about having to give her favorite CD to a friend, regardless of the fact how much she loved the songs. She later realized that CD blessed her friend tremendously and herself by giving up her favorite CD. When I read about the gift of the CD I felt the present of The Holy Spirit very strongly and I would get a song of my own.

At my church that Sunday morning, a young lady minister was praying a powerful prayer and in that prayer she became prophetic and said someone would need to surrender there all to Christ Jesus when the doors of the church were open and there was an alter call. That service from alter prayer throughout, The Holy Ghost continued to touch me and feel me with His presence, so much so I couldn't control my tears. I can truly confess that HE SPEAKS THROUGH OUR DREAMS.

SCRIPTURE:

I Samuel 1:11 (NIV) And she made vow, saying, "O Lord Almighty, if you will only look upon your servant's misery and remember me, and not forget your servant but give her a son, then I will give him to the Lord for all the days of his life, and no razor shall ever be used on his head."

TRANSLATION:

Be careful what you promise in prayer because God may take you up on it. Although we are not in a position to barter with God, he may still choose to answer a prayer that has an attached promise.

I love my Lord and Savior, Jesus the Christ. If we honestly seek Him, He can be found. As a matter of fact, I believe he goes to and fro in the earth, and he is available. At the alter, the young minister had given a word and it followed me back to my seat, surrender all, I took out my hymnal and went to the directory and there it was, "I surrender all," and The Lord had kept His promise and given me my song. This happens on Easter Sunday, April, two thousand and seven.

We need to learn more on how to hear from The Holy Spirit, and writer Lysa Teskeurst recommends five methods on how to hear from The Holy Spirit. 1.) Does what I am hearing line up with the Scriptures? 2.) Is it consistent with God's character? 3.) Is it being confirmed through messages, what I am hearing at church or studying in my quiet time? 4.) Is it beyond me? 5.) Would it please God? This is the litmus test.

This scripture convicted me very strongly when I read Acts 19:6, "And when Paul had laid hands upon them, the Holy Ghost came on them; and they spake with tongues, and prophesied."

This was a special gifting of The Holy Spirit, this will be recorded on The Staff as a special time and event.

Romans 6:13 (NIV) Do not offer parts of your body to sin, instruments of wickedness, but rather offer yourselves to God, as those who have been brought from death to life, and offer the parts of your body to him as instruments of righteousness.

TRANSLATION:

Avoid letting any part of our bodies be used as tools of wrong doing, which is a sin against God. Jesus Christ's sacrifice on the cross gave us life, back from death, and we want to be tools in the hands of God, to be used in good purposes. We are no longer tied to the law, where sin enslaves you, but you are free under God's favor and mercy.

Chapter Six

THE BLESSED GIFTS

Acts 19:6 (NIV) And when Paul had laid hands upon them, the Holy Ghost came on them; and they spake with tongues and prophesied.

TRANSLATION:

When Paul laid his hands on these disciples, they received the Holy Spirit, just as the disciples had at Pentecost, resulting in outward visible signs of the Holy Spirit's presence. We are to seek to share our faith with others, and allow the Holy Spirit to give you whatever experiences he thinks you need. When I read Acts 19:6, I was convicted by it very strongly and I felt led by the Holy Spirit to believe this blessed gift was for me. I now have His Authority to lay hands on others in the name of Jesus Christ, and the Jesus Christ will bless according to his will.

When the Holy Spirit makes that unique call and informs you, or someone else, that we have been called by the Holy Spirit of God to become his servant, whom he will train and prepare us for the purpose that we are called to from the beginning by

God. Those he calls he equips, so we must ready ourselves for his teaching to become that worthy servant that the Holy Spirit desires to trust with his word. The Lord will teach us through His Word, witnesses our prayers and we will be convicted by them. I often got messages wrong on what I was supposed to do and failed and was chastised for it. I am so thankful for the Holy Spirit when he chastised us; he does not give us what we deserve, those whom he loves he chastens. In the Word a father disciplines his children because he loves them and wants them to go in the right direction. The father is held accountable to the Lord to teach his children the right way to live. The teaching that must go forward when we are called into the ministry for our Lord Jesus Christ. We must begin to make changes in our attitudes, be mindful of our conduct, the company we keep, and we should avoid the places that we used to frequent. To walk in right pathways with Christ, He will lead, guide and teach us his right pathway to walk in his righteousness. We will learn that we can't talk about people in negative ways, the language that we used daily must be spoken with respect and humility.

We must know, that when life and health issues come after us, we will learn about the great love that the Lord has for us. We can call his name in our prayers and tell him about while we need him in our circumstances. While pending this to others, I can look back on how The Lord kept me, because of his love and not my being worthy of his care, healing and strengthening me.

Chapter Seven

CALL TO PRAYER AND FASTING

Matthew 11:15 (NIV) He who has ears let him hear.

THIS FAST STARTED ON Saturday April 07, 2007, because the Holy Spirit reminded me I had done something wrong and I had been moved to repent through fasting and prayer. The Holy Spirit encouraged me to fasting and prayer to correct my mistakes.

As I looked on my pass mistakes, I realized that I need to trust my life to the Lord, and through this 9-day fast, I made declaration to give my life over to Christ Jesus, and were willing to learn how to be led by The Holy Spirit. In the word, the Lord said I didn't love Him now, the way I did in the past. I am learning to be obedient to his word and let The Holy Spirit direct my path.

The Scriptures says, "He that hath ears to hear, let him hear." Matthew 11:15, I want to hear what you desire to say to me, Lord God, help me to hear clearly what you are saying to me, so I may hear and perceive what your word says from the scriptures and obey your word. I pray for discernment to hear and obey through the blessing of Jesus Christ. I am praying to come into right alignment with God's Will.

Minister Stanley in Walking Wisely, teaches when we fail to heed God's Prompting, confess that we made a mistake or a sin against God. Receive His forgiveness, then take a second and ask the question, why did I fail to heed this prompting from The Holy Spirit? In the future, act immediately on what I felt The Holy spirit was telling to me to do, this will help us to grow with confidence and to hear and act immediately.

We need to be seeking and observing events in the world so we can witness the righteous hand of our mighty God in order to grow, seek out and learn from Wise People, because he who walks with wise people will be wise. Seeking Wise Counsel will help us to avoid walking through life alone, to spend time with people who have been through experiences that we have faced and will be facing. Spend time with people who have succeeded in areas of life in which we would like to participate. Lord will you reveal to me the errors and sins of my ways, so I can find forgiveness and Repentance in the name of Jesus.

This is unfortunate we fail so often, trying to get it right; for us to be children of God and learn to be led by the Holy Spirit in doing our work in the building of the Kingdom.

Matthew 11:15 (NIV) He who has ears let him hear.

TRANSLATION:

God tells us, if there were ever a time to listen to his voice, the time is now, be willing to listen and repent and be restored.

Chapter Eight

ALL POWER BELONGS TO GOD

SIS. JOHNSON

Psalm 89:18 (NIV) Indeed, our shield belongs to the Lord, our king to the Holy One of Israel.

PROPHETESS JOHNSON CALLED AND said, she was on the way, she had a word for me and my friend who was visiting us from out of town for a few days. This word will bring clarity and encouragement and some assurances from the Lord, who hears her prayers. She later explained she was led by the Holy Spirit to talk with her and fully explain that the Lord has called her to ministry. There was an immediate agreement with our friend from out of town acknowledged that she already knew ministry is her calling. My young friend from out of town shared a powerful move of the Lord how he is using her. Some mornings very early she is dressing for work, while she is at her vanity and mirror, a name would appear in writing in the mirror, in the beginning, it was frightening, our experiences grows us and gives us strength and we received the message and deliver it with power and authority from on high. She realizes, the Lord is speaking, and someone has been praying for an answer, today she will provide, the Lord is trusting her to raise up a standard, to help heal a wounded warrior.

The Holy Spirit was speaking to Prophetess Johnson that evening, she said that the Holy Spirit said I had an important message for her, concerning her best friend and we were praying for a resolution that the Lord would provide. I began to speak information that I had to know knowledge off; I said to Prophetess Johnson, you want your friend to acknowledge your ministry the Lord has called you to. You are already preaching, and now the Lord wants me to anoint you with the power of prophecy, the Lord has given you great power with insight and revelation, walk in your blessing from the Lord. The Lord is saying we won't let any hindrances, lack of support, downgrades what the Lord has done. Be encouraged, the battle isn't yours, and it belongs to the Lord. This was our take away from this move of the Lord; the Lord always provides for those who believe what he is doing in our lives. If you don't entertain battles on the home front, we can't learn to stand on the Lord and His promises. The Lord said to me, "Stand on my Word," in my vision, I saw the Bible passed before my eyes, I still deliver.

The presence of the Holy Spirit was flowing between us, so strongly that I could hardly believe what the Spirit was saying between us. She asked me, would you help me, of course, I will, remembering the prayers and follow-up, not letting me backslide when I didn't fully understand what the Lord was saying in the early 2006 and 2007, I was in discovery weekly with fasting, Bible Study, home, and church. You gave me great support, and now the Lord told you, get Oscar's to help. The first time I saw you, you were next door anointing someone home and praying for all the family within the house, the Lord had sent you to own that mission. I saw you through the window, I went out and introduced myself, and you prayed for me and didn't even know my name while visiting my hometown. I said yes, I felt the Holy Spirit, after your anointed prayers, I believe at that moment, the Lord had blessed our friendship.

ALL POWER BELONGS TO GOD: Sis Johnson

Psalm 89:18 (NIV) Indeed, our shield belongs to the Lord, our King to the Holy One of Israel.

TRANSLATION:

Without God's help, we are weak and powerless, inadequate for even the simplest spiritual task. But when we are filled with God's spirit, his power flows through us, and our accomplishments will exceed our expectations.

Chapter Nine

EMBRACE GOD'S LOVE: SPIRITUAL ATTACKS

James 1:12 (NIV) Blessed is the man who perseveres under trials, because when we has stood the test, he will receive the crown of life that God has promised to those who love him.

WHEN THE HOLY SPIRIT brings people together and teaches us how to become intercessors with others, I glorify God for His love and trust and his great patience with me. My friend called late Sunday night and she told me of this problem concerning believing a property that had issues needing to be resolved. She said she may need to sue to clear the problem up.

I believe the Holy Spirit prompted me to tell her to read the 23 Psalm and to use it each time she has an encounter or meeting with others or her lawyers. When I told my friend this, I felt The Holy Spirit. This was resolved without any further legal action on her part; the other party called and resolved the issue.

Earlier Sunday, I was in my church and our excellent pastor put forth a sermon that the Holy Ghost spoke to me through. Our pastor preached "more bark than bite" and the Holy Ghost was very present and powerful in me through the preached word. Our Pastor made these comments that we have come of repasts, so prepare for a long and rigorous journey. We are being prepared for God to take us some place and we will need all our strength, energy and faith for the journey. Remembering the opposite of fear is love. There is nothing we can do against the love that God has for us but embrace it and grow. When fear comes upon us, recall all that Jesus Christ has done in our past in our life so we can be prepared to fight the enemy. When I wrote this, the Holy Spirit was so convicting, it drew me to tears.

The Word was telling me through the Holy Spirit to expect greater levels of attacks in my spiritual journey and with that authority, comes higher levels of the enemy. I am to remember the way to the heart of God is on my knees.

This is a testimony for someone, I received this over two years ago and I am able to testify through my prayers, and from many, many others' situations in my life. The love of God, for me, has kept me through all the storms, mistakes, short-comings, He continues to keep me. I am revealing my testimonies because the Holy Spirit tells me through my testimonies others will be renewed, restored, made whole, through His word. I don't know where those spoken words will take me as I write this in September, 2010, to God be the Glory for he is worthy to be praised.

EMBRACE GOD'S LOVE:

James 1:12 (NIV) Blessed is the man who perseveres under trials, because when he has stood the test, he will receive the crown of life that God has promised to those who love him.

TRANSLATION:

God's crown of life is not glory and honor here on earth, but the reward of eternal life, living with God forever. Temptation comes from evil desires inside us, not from God. It begins with an evil, though, and becomes sin when we dwell on the thought and allow it to become an action. The more we give way to sin, the greater the destruction will take place in us. We must not let it begin, cancel the lie immediately, and call the devil a liar. Tell Satan the Word of God is against you.

Chapter Ten

THE BLESSING OF GOD

Jude 1:20 (KJV) But ye, beloved, building up yourselves on your most holy faith, praying in the Holy Ghost.

WHEN THE HOLY SPIRIT is preparing you, we must learn to be obedient, because the Holy Spirit is always looking to grow us into the purpose planned for our lives in the foreknowledge before the beginning of time. We were always in His plan to do a great work in taking the gospel to all the nations. I am looking back on the many people that the Holy Spirit brought into my life with words and direction from the Lord that will prepare me for the next level.

I received a call from my friend, and there is a word from the Lord she proposed and gave me Jude 1:20 and from this you will be blessed to speak in tongues in due time. When this scripture was given and I read it, I was convicted by the prompting of the Holy Spirit. The Holy Spirit tells me when I pray through the Holy Ghost, He will bless me with greater authority and power. Look not left nor right, but keep my eyes on God on high, this will also be the answer to the enemy. This was repeated by her that I would get release and I began speaking in tongues.

There is a Care Center I visit often, two or three times a week, and there are several patients I visit and pray for each time I come, with the spirit of the Lord about me. There were two roommates that had their faculty about them clearly and were very spiritual. One of them suffered with tremendous pain in her eye and hand and I would pray profoundly for relief for her. On one occasion while praying, she reached out and grasped my hand and the anointing was upon her and she replied, she got relief. That night, I talked with Prophetess Johnson about my visit and the pain that the ladies were having and she suggested to buy pure white handkerchiefs and face towels, bless them and give them   to those that were in need. That very message had been preached by a minister very recently and once again I felt convicted by the prompting of The Holy Spirit that I can do this, as Paul and Peter used the sweat rags from their faces when they were preaching and would throw them down and someone would pick them up and were healed from using their sweat rags, and the prompting of the Holy Spirit said I could do the same and He would bless my works in His Holy name.

Receiving a gift from God is a special blessing and is noteworthy to be recorded on The Staff.

THE BLESSING OF GOD:

Jude 1:20 (KJV) But ye, beloved, building up yourselves on your most holy faith, praying in the Holy Ghost.

TRANSLATION:

We must build up our lives ever more strongly upon the foundation of our holy faith, learning to pray in the power and strength of the Holy Spirit.

Chapter Eleven

THE GIFT OF A VISIONARY

John 14:12 (NIV) I tell you the truth, anyone who has faith in me will do what I have been doing. He will do even greater things than these, because I am going to the Father.

ON SUNDAY, THE 11:00 am service our pastor preached on Moses and his staff that was anointed of God, and that some of us already have what we need to go out and do the things that God has called us to do. The pastor went on to say that we are standing on a miracle. While the pastor was speaking, the Holy Spirit was very strong on me. I always try to be very observant to pastors' sermons because I have gotten messages in the past through his powerful preaching.

I made a call to my friend in Tuskegee, on Sunday night in effect, I was returning his call from Saturday. We talked for a while, then we had prayer and he said the Holy Spirit told him, "I had the gift of a Visionary." And my "Gifts will make Room for me." My friend said, I don't know what it means, but the Holy Spirit wanted you to know that.

On May 11, 2008, a minister was preaching and he said those that have a long-term Vision, God will bless them that they may have grace to share what they've seen, no telling how long. This coincided with what my friend had said on Sunday night that I was a "Visionary."

As I started to write this I felt the Holy Spirit, in John 14:13 and whatsoever ye asked in my name, that will I do, that the Father may be glorified in the Son. We are agents of Christ, sent into the mission fields to do greater works in the name of Jesus Christ, that he may receive, all the glory and honor that is due his name.

We are in our growing stages, applying that which we know and understand; this shall be recorded on The Staff Ministry, that God calls us to a ministry in His name, that we may fulfill that which he has purposed in our lives from the beginning.

THE GIFTS OF A VISIONARY

JOHN 14:12 (NIV) I tell you the truth, anyone who has faith in me will do what I have been doing. He will do even greater things than these, because I am going to the Father.

TRANSLATION:

Jesus is not saying that his disciples would do more amazing miracles; after all, raising the dead is about as amazing as you can get. The disciples are working through the power of the Holy Spirit, and will carry the gospel of God throughout the whole world.

Chapter Twelve

ALL THINGS THROUGH CHRIST

Psalms 23:1 The Lord is my Shepherd, I shall not be in want.

IT WAS HEARD AND follows with enthusiasm when it was discovered Apostle Paul would sweat tremendously, and unknowingly would throw away his sweaty, wet handkerchief and someone in the midst of the gathering would pick up the handkerchief and use it on the areas of their sickness and be healed. Truly the presence of the Lord is upon us and this teaches us, we can become Christ-like. In developing the character likeness of The Christ, we must dedicate time to spend with Him, study our Bible to show ourselves approved that the Word of God is our life. We will never be perfect, but the Holy Spirit will lead us into right pathways and with his anointing and authority to do works through the Holy Spirit.

Paul would be praying and preaching and he had sweat rags (handkerchiefs) that he used when he prayed and worked himself into a sweat, and he would give it to someone with an illness and they were healed.

When hearing the word preached on the great works of Paul and how the sweat rags became a healing force that goes on even in today's society, though not widely acknowledged, I felt the unction of the Holy Spirit saying to me through the ministers preaching that I can do the same. Having experienced this twice, I now believed the Holy Spirit had blessed me with the gift of towel and handkerchief to bless others in need.

My visit to the Care Center home, there were two wonderful friends at the Care Center. Each had good memory and speech; this made it easy to share the scriptures that we selected. Their wisdom in the word was very rewarding for me on a number of occasions and The Holy Spirit would speak to me from their wise sayings. During the visits, I witnessed the pain and suffering on each of them in their own situation; there was a lady in tremendous pain and medication was of little value. She had suffering areas continually on her and I prayed many prayers for the decrease in their discomforts.

Perhaps this was one of the immediate implementing's of the handkerchief gifts, that I anointed and prayed for the benefits of the Gifts of Handkerchief for my friends. The benefit was rewarding, there were fewer complaints and less indication of the pain. Next was someone that was in need of oxygen twenty-four hours a day and seven days a week, her health had declined considerably each time I would come and the daughter would be there and was appreciative of the prayer and her mother's favorite scripture read. I would read the 23rd Psalm for her and the benefit was very nourishing, and rewarding for her.

I was in prayer home early one morning and I am fairly certain she and others at Care Center were in my prayers. While I was praying, I heard prayer cloth for my friend that used oxygen every hour of every day. My next visit, I had anointed the handkerchief and brought it with me. When I arrived at her room she had several family members in the small room. I went next door to the two friend's room. One said to me, she heard the lady next door was very weak and would pass soon. I took a second look and there were more family members outside her room as well. I entered her room and offered prayer and her favorite 23rd Psalm to her and she nodded yes. As I welcomed the Holy Ghost to help me pray the prayer that would help someone, so it was, I heard in my spirit to give her my breath and the word was so strong to me I prayed the blessing of the Holy Spirit of God upon her for health and strength.

The next time I came, I placed the handkerchief on her chest and blessed it. I'm not certain exactly how much longer she lived, I believe it was over a week later, which gave more family members time to come to town and spend time with her. The daughter was so appreciate of the time I had come to her with prayer and scripture.

Our Lord is due all the praise and honor with worship that we can bring to His precious name for the Lord is worthy.

ALL THINGS THROUGH CHRIST: (Sweat Rag)

The Lord is my Shepherd, I shall not be in want.

TRANSLATION:

Psalm 23:1 (NIV) As the Lord is the good Shepherd, so we are his sheep — not frightened, passive animals, but obedient followers, wise enough to follow one who will lead us in the right places and in the right ways. When we recognize the good Shepherd and become that disciple, he is calling us to be, follow him and do greater works that he has called us to.

Chapter Thirteen

THE LORD GIVES US DREAMS

GIDEON—YOUR GIFTS

Judges 6:18 (NIV) "Please do not go away until I come back and bring my offering and set it before you." And the Lord said, "I will wait until you return."

I REMEMBER THE TREMENDOUS efforts my friend and I employed to try and get the company documents to operate his business and the workers to do the documentation and maintain everyday business. We realized very early from losing customers, my friend had only two small mini-buses and the customers were looking for good equipment with courteous drivers and excellent service. My prayers went out continually for the Holy Spirit to bless Oscar Lee with the coaches he needed and everything else. This would mean employees, drivers and office support. I was looking to the Holy Spirit for everything in prayer.

He ordered his first coach, and the loan officers continually asked for more documentation before they would sign off. I had a talk with them in which I explained they had all the paperwork needed for this purchase. That night, I went to prayer specifically for the Holy Spirit to move and touch, right hearts and minds to sign the paperwork, so we could move forward as a tour company scheduling trips.

Our God answers prayer if we believe and trust Him. Early Friday morning in my dream, I looked at what would be our clock sitting on the dresser with red numbers and it gave me what turned out to be scriptures 7:6-18. I examine the numbers carefully; the numbers only matched up to the Old Testament. The scripture read that Gideon was called up from the barn chaffing wheat; he met this stranger that told him the Lord had called him to lead an army. Gideon thought certainly not him, he was considered the least in the family. We are all Gideons until we give our life over to Christ Jesus and commit ourselves to be led by the Holy Spirit, and we will testify the great things the Holy Spirit has done through us in our lives. I wondered what this vision meant. The Lord said, "Call Rev. Fred your brethren, he spoke with authority to the vision. You do not need to wait for your answer, God will supply. Get in your car and meet with your appointment, we have cell phones." Thank God for brethren's in Christ.

The Holy Spirit quickened our answer. I was on my way to Tuskegee later that morning and my cell phone rang. My son told me the purchase was approved. I said thank you Lord for teaching me to trust you, and this testimony is also to address the needs of others the same way; just when it seemed like there was no hope, the Holy Ghost reached out and touched the hard-heart of someone standing in the way of a blessing from the Lord. What God has for us, no man has the power to prevent it from coming to fruition, and all God's children said, Amen.

THE LORDS GIVES US DREAMS

> Judges 6:18 (NIV) "Please do not go away until I come back and bring my offering and set it before you." And the Lord said, "I will wait until you return."

TRANSLATION:

The Lord promised Gideon, I will be with you, and give you the strength you need to overcome the opposition. In spite of this clear promise of strength, Gideon made excuses. Seeing only his limitation and weaknesses, he failed to see how God could work through him. We aren't to spend time doubting, instead spend our time doing the assignments the Lord set before us, because He has already promised to be with us.

Chapter Thirteen

HIS LOVE: OSCAR

Isaiah 57:18 (NIV) I have seen his ways, but I will heal him; I will guide him and restore comfort to him.

WHEN WE WAKE IN the morning, always have a reason to thank the Holy Spirit for the night of covering, giving us not only the opportunity to thank Him but to ask Him to lead us, go before us and establish our going that we may be in the right places for His assignments. In this intervention by the Holy Spirit, He is our ever-present help, we should be seeking to serve Him by helping others and He will be in our midst.

March 17, 2009, Rev. Horace was preaching from his Faith Church and he made this powerful statement referencing the relationship between King David and Jesus Christ. He said David is a man who we know has been in the presence of God. Rev. Horace says Jesus said that, like David, we can pray and drive demons away. When I heard that, I felt the prompting of the Holy Spirit, so I wrote it down because I didn't understand what it meant fully. I encountered this note again on March 29, 2009. I read it and felt the Holy Spirit again, and I have been praying in that authority long before now, because others have called and asked me to pray for them; however, receiving the call reinforces me with authority through the Holy Spirit that He is giving me greater authority to use His name to help others.

July 4, 2010, a friend and I were having intercessory prayer, and as he was praying, he said pray for Julia, Oscar is going away. This disturbed me, because I felt the Holy Spirit, and I don't know what that means, whether good or not so good. However, I am to remember I said yes to the Lord, and I promised to do His assignments.

On September 21, 2010, I received this information about our characters, that it refers to who I am, not what I do. It was stated because of the character Joseph displayed, his story was recorded. So the question we're asked is, will your character require that your story be preserved for future generations? When I read this, I felt the prompting of the Holy Spirit that I would produce something that would be recorded and remembered for the future.

When we were saved, God knew from our end, that He had a purpose for our lives. God transfers His grace (His Anointing) upon us. Expect attacks from the enemy because he knows from the spiritual realms that the Holy Spirit has placed His Anointing upon you, and before you know what happened, God has made me forget my mind. He has moved me into my blessing. When I heard this, I felt The Holy Spirit very strongly. The Love of God can't be compared to anything that is in existence. He forgives us of our sins, and continue to grow us. He knows us better than we know ourselves; "His Love" never ceases.

Even today family, I fight the good fight of faith. I'm trying to keep the devil in the abyss, showing up, trying to interrupt our work assignment. However though the Spirit of adoption, Roman 8:15 we bind the Spirit of Rejection in Jesus Name. Someone is praying for me. Thank You.

THE HOLY SPIRIT SPEAKS:

Isaiah 57:18 (NIV) I have seen his ways, but I will heal him; I will guide him and restore comfort to him.

TRANSLATION:

Those of us who are humble and repentant of our sins and wrong doings, the high and Holy God promises to save us because it is impossible for us to go up to His level to save ourselves. The great compassion of our Lord allows Him to continue to grows us according to His will.

Chapter Fourteen

FROM MY STICK, TO GOD'S STAFF I

Jeremiah 29:11 (NIV) "For I know the plans I have for you," declares the Lord, "plans to prosper you and not to harm you, plans to give you hope and a future."

I WAS DRIVING OUT to visit my dear friend at a Care Facility. On the way out I was listing to Minister Paul on my CDs collection I had purchased. On one of the CDs, there were preaching about Moses and his staff. Preacher was saying this isn't a stick, but a staff that had been blessed for a purpose. I heard this in my spirit and the Holy Spirit came upon me and drew me to tears. I didn't understand what I had received, then a thought ran across my mind, and it said, "Your Moses Stick." I was flooded with tears: Lord, you mean that old hickory stick that I keep in my prayer room and walk with wherever I go? I selected it over four years ago when I cut down this beautiful hickory tree, and cut this solid and sound walking pole.

My brother who is a reverend came over Saturday evening, and I told him the story about the stick now being a Staff, called by the Holy Spirit; I wanted him to anoint it. When he began to anoint the staff, it became very hot in his hand. He was rubbing the oil on the upper position of the stick. He said, Oscar, feel the heat on the stick. At first I didn't feel any heat, then it came through. This was unimagined, standing there outside the house oiling that stick, and it was registering more heat.

When I left my brother, I continued to my next Care Center. As I was finishing my rounds, I saw a young mother with two young girls, perhaps 8 or 9 and 11 or 13 years old with their mother, braiding their grandmother's hair, who was in the Care Center. As I spoke to the girls and their mother, I felt the presence of the Holy Spirit, so I began to follow His leading and prayed a special prayer over the children, blessing them especially so for a gift that the Lord had stored up for them. The Holy Spirit was so powerful that His presence went through us, hit a lady sitting in a chair a short distance away, and she began to praise and shout, threw up both arms in the air, bowed her head, perhaps thanking the Lord for answered prayer. I continued over to the lady and blessed her with a fresh anointing of the Holy Ghost. I believe the Holy Spirit had fulfilled her need and she celebrated. I confess, we were on fire that afternoon, for the Lord was our ever-present help, thank you Lord God.

FROM MY STICK, TO GOD'S STAFF

> Jeremiah 29:11 (NIV) "For I know the plans I have for you," declares the Lord, "plans to prosper you, plans to give you hope and a future."

TRANSLATION:

> We are all encouraged by a leader who stirs us to move ahead, someone who believes we can do the task He has given and who will be with us all the way. God is that kind of leader. He knows the future, and His plans for us are good and full of hope. As long as God, who knows the future, provides our agenda and goes with us as we fulfill His mission, we have

boundless hope. This does not mean that we will be spared pain, suffering, or hardship, but that God will see us through to a glorious conclusion.

Chapter Fifteen

BE A BLESSING

Job 22:27-28; You will pray to Him, and He will hear you, and you will fulfill your vows. (28) What you decide on will be done, and light will shine on your ways. (NIV)

I HAVE BEEN IN a storm for my health continually, so I called up a Health Center to come down and renew my vitamin and eating regiment and have blood tests and screening done to get a good understanding of my health. I had two blood draws a week apart, and each time the results were good. My blood count was a few points low and my immune system needed strengthening.

While with the health director, she reviewed my results, and at that time, I felt the presence of the Holy Spirit and I asked her for permission to anoint her buildings and she said yes. Then the Spirit led me to pray for her after, and anoint her and her hands, and the Holy Spirit would bless her with great insight and authority. The Holy Spirit was very powerful during this anointing and this blessing would come upon others and their health would be made better as they entered into the health institute when The Anointing of the Holy Spirit was upon this facility of the Health Center. The entrance to the director's office was also anointed and when he walked through his entrance door The Holy Spirit was upon him.

The Prophecy says under the anointing, he would have more authority and power in his conferences and seminar classes and his teaching will be received in a deeper and more penetrating way. This is a record in The Prophecy Ministry of Oscar in the Health Center and this document is attached to This Staff, called in to Prophecy by The Holy Spirit, and His Presence during this writing brought me to tears. I thank God for His ever-present help.

The date and time and position on The Staff is to follow.

BE A BLESSING

> Job 22: 27-28 (NIV) You will pray to Him, and He will hear you, and you will fulfill your vows. (28) What you decide on will be done, and light will shine on your ways.

TRANSLATION:

> You shall also decide and decree a thing and it shall be established for you; and the light shall shine upon your ways. When we are about to pray a healing prayer, pray a few minutes and be led by the Holy Spirit, to reveal to us the very Words we "decide to pray," which will give us what we want.

Chapter Sixteen

HE INCREASES

John 15:5 (NIV) I am the Vine; you are the branches. If a man remains in me and I in him, he will bear much fruit; apart from me you can do nothing.

I WAS IN THE Health Center for rest and healing, trying to restore a healthy colon. I began with more rest and sleep, and then added a few therapies. I scheduled a lymphatic drainage massage that releases toxins from the body if done properly. It releases blockages and this allows the body to heal itself with a corrected diet and the blessing of the Holy Spirit. He tells us aside from Him, we can do nothing. I went there to rest and build my energy, but the Holy Spirit had other plans: there were workers there, and He wanted to grow and increase their levels of authority through the Holy Spirit; they are to help enhance the building of the Kingdom of God.

Mrs. Reid was recommended as the most qualified to give our bodies the desired attention they needed. When she began to work on me, the Holy Spirit prompted me to anoint her head and hand. He would bless her with authority to do greater works in the name of Jesus Christ our Lord and Savior. I believe the Holy Spirit didn't want her to work on my body until she was anointed to do so. When this was done, she began to work and appeared to be looking at various organs, and described them and began speaking in tongues. She stated that I was filled with the Holy Spirit from head to toe. This was an awesome experience lying there before His mighty presence. Mrs. Reid, my therapist, said when I met her how she loves the Lord and this awesome work the Holy Spirit was guiding her into. After the blessing in the name of the Lord, I could tell immediately the Holy Spirit had just elevated her with spiritual increase and with sight into the body, and the revelation on what she was looking at and hearing the Holy Spirit and spoke in tongues. On Sunday, Mrs. Reid invited me to visit her church and I did, and was prompted by the Holy Spirit to pray blessing on the pastor. This minister was a powerful woman of the Holy Spirit and could pray, sing, and preach. She also would receive the increase that only the Lord can give. I heard in my spirit, this church is for training, to prophecy this training is preparation for what He has for her, she will become a powerful minister. She will have increased authority in her prayers and her right hand has blessings upon it, and in her ministry when she prays and preaches there will be more healing and more lives coming to Christ Jesus, through her ministry. The children are so important to her, as I looked at the involvement they have in the church with the youth minister.

This is prophecy ministry of Oscar, Sr in the Health Center and this document will be attached to This Staff, called into Prophecy by The Holy Spirit. There will be a recording on the Staff.

HE INCREASES

> John 15:5 (NIV) I am the Vine; you are the branches. If a man remains in me and I in him, he will bear much fruit; apart from me you can do nothing.

TRANSLATION:

> If we are to remain in Christ Jesus, we must become believers, doing what God says, become followers of His, and take the Gospel to the community. A Holy and sanctified life

is through Christ Jesus. We are the branch, attached to the Vine, and if we separate from Him, we are helpless and ineffective, because the Word of God isn't in us. If we stay in Christ, we will receive the nourishment and salvation for our souls.

Chapter Sixteen

THE BEYOND

Ephesians 1:4 (NIV) For he chose us in him before the creation of the world to be holy and blameless in his sight.

I WAS HAVING A dream this morning, about 06:45, when I saw this little knitted mat, very colorful with a background that looked to be a field of beautiful flowers, and this fence around all the flowers, and a gate to enter into the field. When the small hand-sized mat spiraled towards me, this mat became a lasso that twirled into this large field of flowers and grass that was fenced in, and this was a beautiful landscape. I believe I approached the gate to climb over the fence. I was trying to realize, what is this about? I looked at the little mat, lassoed into a word, "The Beyond," then the scenery changed from the beautiful flowery looking field of this vision into this: if you will, "The Beyond" that I saw was as if I were in a space capsule headed into outer space in a strange-looking and uncharacteristic space, going up in a spiraling flight. It looked like the top side of the earth, the round portion, and as I saw this, more light began to appear and the pathway was narrowing as I looked over the top of it, and there was this hugeness and vastness that was before me; there was no dream in me that would have allowed me to witness a flash into the mysteries of the Lord. All this space had me looking with deep interest to try and gather what this was all about. I knew I was viewing the outer realms, where it was dark, appearing into more light, looking over the top, but in the distance were brighter lights, piercing down and cutting into the darkness in the distance, but nothing was clear enough for understanding. While trying to see more, I woke myself up, amazed, at what I had just witnessed.

AT THIS TIME, I got up and wrote down this most unusual vision, how it transpired, and the questions what does it really mean and is it for the future. I was explaining my dream to my friend concerning what I saw and wondering what it meant. Fred spoke powerfully to this vision and what it represented in scripture, and having authority that only the Holy Spirit can give to those He has called unto Himself, for His assignments. I felt confidence in his interpretation, as he has been a man in ministry for over twenty years and he keeps his hands on the gospel plow. While writing this last statement, I felt the presence of the Holy Spirit.

WHOM THE HOLY SPIRIT has given authority to, when the Lord blesses the anointing, it is unlimited. This is what the reverend's interpretation of the dream means.

THE BEYOND

> Ephesians 1:4 (NIV) For he chose us in him before the creation of the world to be holy and blameless in his sight.

TRANSLATION:

> God "chose us in him" to let us know that salvation depends on God and not us, that God graciously and freely gives salvation. We can't influence God's decision to save us; he saves us according to his plan.

God chose us, and when we belong to him through Jesus Christ, God looks at us as if we have never sinned. All we can do is express our thanks for his wonderful love.

Chapter Seventeen

SOW A SEED OF FAITH

Malachi 3:8 (NIV) Will a man rob God? Yet you rob me, "But you ask, 'How do we rob you.'" In tithes and offering.

I WAS READING PREVIOUS notes on sowing seeds for harvest. I read the statement that I prepared for my church mortgage liquidation assignment. When I read the first verse I felt the presence of the Holy Spirit.

"We must sow seed in order to have a harvest; not just any seeds, but seeds of faith that you are a believer and trust God, that He will provide a fruitful harvest." When I read this, I remembered earlier, on October 20, 2010, when reading the Bible, I read upon this scripture and the Holy Spirit touched me and I wrote Malachi 3:8-10, will a man rob God? I thought with my tithes and offering, and first fruits with seed-sowing gifts, I was doing the right thing, but the Holy Ghost spoke in October 2010, and I have learned to act positive, because the Holy Spirit is totally righteous and I must quickly correct my errant thinking. We can imagine a powerful word that questions your gift giving, tithes and offering with a Statement, "Will a Man Rob God." I gathered my thoughts and prepared gifts to small churches that I know and mailed them off promptly.

I thought my robbing my savior was resolved, but I was asked to provide a seed offering of Faith that you are a believer and trust God that He will provide a Fruitful Harvest. I know the Lord is my provider, that what I have, belongs to Him. I asked in my prayers what were the correct funds to contribute, and I received the answer, and to further inform me, in my vision that morning I heard a voice say, I want my gift now. With this kind of confirmation, I visited the post office and mailed off my gifts to the churches, from that very day, from the voice into my spirit.

Trusting the Holy Spirit to lead us and trusting the Lord has our best interest is most important on our spiritual journey, for without faith, it is impossible to please God. I received phone calls, and one of the pastors was so thankful, I believe he was in tears for the First Fruit Gift he had received. The first gift he received, he thought that it may have been his confirmation that his prayers had been answered. He asked his congregation for that amount, individually to support mortgage debt elimination.

Right now, I am believing why the Holy Spirit needed His gift was because there are churches in need of our gifts, while going through these difficult times, and we must trust the Holy Spirit to lead us and guide us into the right places to be that which the Lord has called us to be.

A few months later, I was in a church. The service had ended and I was on line to shake the minister's hand. When I finally reached him and thanked him for his powerful sermon, he said brother, you don't know how much you helped the church with your gift, I thank you for your gift you sent us. I knew he was talking about how the expenses of the church were barely being met and my financial gift helped the church meet a few obligations. I met with a Prophetess a few weeks later and I told her about the Bible quote, "Will a man rob God?" She replied so very strongly to me as she wrote this note to me stating, "The Holy Ghost said the Lord knows you won't rob Him, he knew you would respond quickly to His asking and you met the needs with your gifts to the location you sent them." When I read this tonight, 11/30/11 at 20:50, I felt the unction of the Holy

Spirit when I read again "will a man rob God." I am asking the Holy Spirit in my prayers, have I taken funds from him or have my sins characterized me as taking from my Lord and Savior? I can only ask forgiveness of my sins, for I am in repentance.

SOW A SEED OF FAITH: SCRIPTURE:

> Malachi 3:8 (NIV) Will a man rob God? Yet you rob me, "But you ask, 'How do we rob you.'" In tithes and offering.

TRANSLATION:

> The people of Malachi's day ignored God's command to give a tithe of their income to his temple. They may have feared losing what they had worked so hard to get, but in that, they misjudged God. "Give and it will be given to you." In Luke 6:38, when we give we must remember that the blessings God promises are not always material and may not be experienced completely here on earth, but we will certainly receive them in our future life with Him.

The single most important lesson we need to learn is, whatever we possess, it all belongs to the Lord.

Chapter Eighteen

OUR MISSION CORNER

Isaiah 54:17 (KJV) No weapon formed against thee shall prosper; and every tongue that shall rise against thee in judgment thou shalt condemn. This is the heritage of the servants of the Lord, and their righteous is of me, saith the Lord

AFTER I LEFT SERVICE at church, I went to downtown Atlanta to Our Mission Corner where I met with our friends that are in storms like many of us. I confessed to those that I was praying and preaching to that I needed to be there on this corner with them. I explained to them that the Lord called me to this work and if I didn't go and preach to all the children I encountered, I must be responsible to the Holy Spirit, who blesses me with assignments. I confess, it is a blessing and a gift for the Holy Spirit to call us to preach His word.

I spoke to them about Isaiah 54:17, which states that no weapon formed against us can prosper if we are in right alignment and know who our Savior is. We must confess with our mouth, that Jesus Christ is our Savior, that we are to submit to Him only and be saved. I said we need to return to our homes, give some or receive forgiveness and move on with our lives, because the Holy Spirit is waiting for us to say yes. We all have purpose to fulfill in our lives, if we are going to be ready when Jesus returns for His church.

To one young man I spoke to, I suggested that he should return home and repair his life and move forward. At the end of my speaking, he spoke out and said he felt changed. I said to all of them, when we confess with our mouth we are changed and the transformation begins then. We can later locate a house of worship to serve and become part of the fellowship within the church and the community and become that servant the Lord call us to.

OUR MISSION CORNER:

Isaiah 54:17 (KJV) No weapon formed against thee shall prosper; and every tongue that shall rise against thee in judgment thou shalt condemn. This is the heritage of the servants of the Lord, and their righteous is of me, saith the Lord.

TRANSLATION:

When we think on the Holy Spirit, we acknowledge that he is our redeemer when we give our life to Him and trust him with our total being. The enemies that comes against us will not succeed, and you will have justice against every courtroom lie. The Holy Spirit says, this is the blessing I have given you says the Lord.

Chapter Nineteen

SHARE THE GIFT

I PETER 4:10 (NIV) Each one should use whatever gift he has received to serve others, faithfully administering God's grace in its various forms.

IN THE EARLY GROWTH in our spiritual lives, we are trying to learn how we are led by the Holy Spirit. I remind others, this is a journey, in the lesson of how to be led by the Holy Spirit. We are continually engaged in prayer, fasting and studying the Bible.

Today, I witness on Our Mission Corner, for the Holy Spirit and the need for His children to hear and be obedient to His word. I spoke to them about "Nourishment For Our Souls," and what it means to seek the Lord for redemption and finding salvation. We spend unaccountable time looking for food, wine and milk for nourishment, the Holy Spirit asks us to seek, listen and obey Him and He would bless us with salvation. He says it is free, it costs us nothing but the promise to serve Him only and be made over. I anointed each of them that were close by, and gave them prophecy for there lives, and the time is now.

Today was a very powerful day. I left the Mission Corner and visited The Care Center where my oldest friend resides. When I walked into the lounge area, my friend saw me, and the others are aware when I come, we have prayer and they receive the blessing the Holy Spirit has for them.

When I arrived home, it looked to be the end of a long day, but shortly after, our niece arrived with her three children. Immediately, the middle baby ran up to me and hugged me. She is only 7 or 8, and while hugging, something urged me to bless her.

I explained to her how the impartation works. I told her the Holy Spirit blessed me with a gift, and I promised the Lord I would share my gift with others. I explained when we hugged, I blessed her and she can bless others, by sharing the word of blessing from the Lord. At that moment, her older sister was carrying the baby inside the house, and her sister turned and hugged her and said, "I blessed you and the baby." To my surprise, I felt the prompting of the Holy Spirit very strongly. I was overwhelmed how the presence of the Holy Spirit touched me, when we shared His gifts with others. Family, this the message of the cross, to love one another as He has loved us, with all your heart, mind, soul, and strength.

SHARE THE GIFT

> I PETER 4:10; Each one should use whatever gift he has received to serve others, faithfully administering God's grace in its various forms.

TRANSLATION:

> Our abilities should be faithfully used in servicing others; none are for our own exclusive enjoyment. Some people, well aware of their abilities, believe that they have the right to use their abilities as they please. Others feel they don't have any special talents at all. Everyone has some gifts; find yours and use them. Peter the Apostle mentions speaking and serving.

As we seek to discover our gifts, if you see a need in the church, seek to meet it. You may discover gifts in areas you might not have guessed.

ABOUT THE AUTHOR

Oscar I. Dixon, Sr.

I was born in Roba, Alabama, August 29, 1942 to Ethel and Rev. Frank D. Dixon, he was a pastor in the Alabama A. M. E. Zion Church Conference. I gave my life to Christ at a very early age, about ten or eleven years old, and were baptized and joined The County Line A. M. E. Zion Church, under the pastorate of Reverend Robert Day.

Through prayer and fasting, I learned, I was called into the ministry at the tender age of fourteen by our Lord, Jesus Christ. As I grew up, I had many encounters from my youth to adulthood, my parents, explained these events, and finally they said we were peculiar children.

I am married, to Mrs. Gloria Allen Dixon, for over 53 years with two children, Oscar Lee and Melinda Rae Dixon Chapman. We are grandparents to Oscar Najee and Natosha Dixon Porter, who gives us two great grands, Imani and Zechariah.

When the Lord called me this time, he got my attention, I had retired from my job, and was in my late fifties. I had built houses and was renovating properties. Doing this time, I became very sick and, I didn't feel so deserving, but the Lord turned my fears into joy. My church family new of my struggles with my health and they prayed without ceasing. I remember my pastor saying to me, brother Oscar, we are praying for you.

Why working on my property, the Lord call my name, He asked me "Will You Serve Me," I said yes and I have not looked back, but sought every opportunity to prepare myself to be able to serve. I took my theology studies from Beacon University, Columbus, Georgia, I achieved my Associate Degree, and Bachelors Degree of Theology. From the Christian Life Studies of Theology, I achieved my Master's Degree of Theology in 2013. I have three years in the The African Methodist Episcopal Zion Church studies.

In 2005, I was invited to come on a mission trip into downtown Atlanta, I am still here working in 2017. I volunteered to work   in two health and rehabilitation facility, I began in 2007 and 2008. There is a take away in this spiritual focus, remember when you pray, believe what you have prayed for, and receive it has though it has already manifested itself, because The Lord answers prayers.

www.ingramcontent.com/pod-product-compliance
Lightning Source LLC
Chambersburg PA
CBHW072205090426
42740CB00012B/2393